THE

DISCIPLESHIP
PROGRAM

WORKBOOK

C. MICHAEL PATTON

TIM KIMBERLEY

CREDO HOUSE

THE DISCIPLESHIP PROGRAM WORKBOOK
© 2011 C. Michael Patton and Timothy G. Kimberley

ISBN: 146115961X
ISBN-13: 978-1461159612

Printed in the United States of America

Credo
House
PUBLISHERS

www.credohouse.org

TABLE OF CONTENTS

OVERVIEW
OF THE
TEN SESSIONS

— • —

1. BIBLE

2. MANKIND

3. TRINITY

4. JESUS

5. FAITH

6. LIVING WITH GOD

7. LIVING WITH THE BIBLE

8. LIVING WITH GOD'S PEOPLE

9. LIVING WITH PAIN

10. LIVING AS LIGHTS

SECTIONS

— • —

GROUNDING YOUR FAITH   GROWING DEEP   DIGGING INTO THE WORD

SESSION 1

BIBLE

ADDITIONAL RESOURCES FOR SESSION 1
AVAILABLE AT DISCIPLESHIPPROGRAM.ORG

GENERAL INTRODUCTION TO THE BIBLE

VITALS:

Canon: The Bible is a collection of 66 books (Protestant).

Time Period: 1400 B.C. – 100 A.D.

Authors: 40+, from fishermen to kings

Language: Hebrew (most of the Old Testament), Aramaic (small portions of the Old Testament), and Koine Greek (New Testament)

The Bible has not been added to in over 2000 years.

"OLD" TESTAMENT VS. "NEW" TESTAMENT

GROWING DEEP

THE BIBLE IS THE "WORD OF GOD"

2 TIM. 3:16–17

"All Scripture is inspired by God and profitable for teaching, for reproof, for correction, for training in righteousness; so that the man of God may be adequate, equipped for every good work."

Five things this tells us about the Bible:

1. It is from God

2. It is to be taught

3. It reproves and corrects our thinking

4. It equips us

5. It does not lack

θεόπνευστος = θεός (theos) πνευστος (pneustos)

Lit. "God breathed"

THE BIBLE IS THE WORD OF MAN

2 PET. 1:20–21

"But know this first of all, that no prophecy of Scripture is a matter of one's own interpretation, for no prophecy was ever made by an act of human will, but men moved by the Holy Spirit spoke from God."

φερόμενοι (pheromenoi)

+ Lit: "to carry," "to bear," "to guide," or "to drive along."

+ Used of a ship being carried by the wind (Acts 27:17).

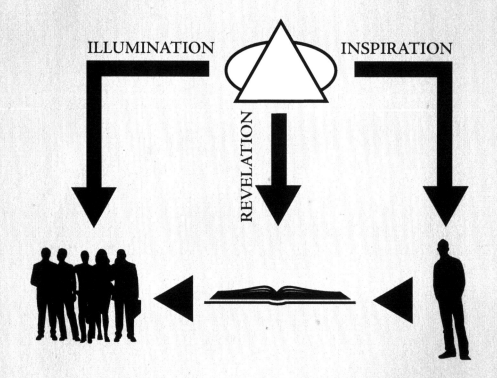

SOLA SCRIPTURA

The Bible is the final and only infallible authority for our faith.

Five primary sources of religious authority:

1. Bible

2. Reason

3. Tradition

4. Experience

5. Emotion

TRADITION:

Religious information that has been handed down to us from various sources.

Examples:

Benefits:

Deficiencies:

REASON:

Information that comes through the human mind's capacity for logical, rational, and analytic thought.

Examples:

Benefits:

Deficiencies:

EXPERIENCE:

Information that comes through direct encounter, participation, or observation.

Examples:

Benefits:

Deficiencies:

EMOTIONS:

Information that comes through subjectively experienced psychological feelings.

Examples:

Benefits:

Deficiencies:

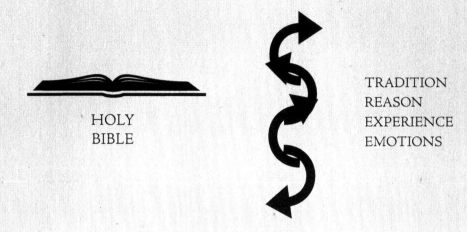

HOLY
BIBLE

TRADITION
REASON
EXPERIENCE
EMOTIONS

ACTS 17:11

These Jews were more open-minded than those in Thessalonica, for they eagerly received the message, examining the Scriptures carefully every day to see if these things were so.

2 TIM. 3:16

"All Scripture is inspired by God and profitable for teaching, for reproof, for correction, and for training in righteousness, that the man of God may be competent, equipped for every good work."

REVELATION 22:18-19

"I warn everyone who hears the words of the prophecy of this book: if anyone adds to them, God will add to him the plagues described in this book, and if anyone takes away from the words of the book of this prophecy, God will take away his share in the tree of life and in the holy city, which are described in this book."

ROM 1:20

For since the creation of the world God's invisible qualities--his eternal power and divine nature--have been clearly seen, being understood from what has been made, so that men are without excuse.

ACTS 17:11

These Jews were more open-minded than those in Thessalonica, for they eagerly received the message, examining the Scriptures carefully every day to see if these things were so.

PHIL. 4:7

And the peace of God, which surpasses all understanding, will guard your hearts and your minds in Christ Jesus.

JOHN 16:8

And when he [the Holy Spirit] comes, he will convict the world concerning sin and righteousness and judgment.

ACT 4:19-20

But Peter and John replied, "Judge for yourselves whether it is right in God's sight to obey you rather than God. For we cannot help speaking about what we have seen and heard."

COFFEE TALK

• Has your understanding of the Bible grown?

• In what ways do you think emotions could conflict with or support the Bible? Give examples.

• Why should we trust Scripture over experience? Give examples where experience would support the Bible.

• Why is tradition dangerous and wonderful?

• If Scripture seems to come in conflict with modern scientific opinion, what should we do? Give examples.

SESSION 2
MANKIND

ADDITIONAL RESOURCES FOR SESSION 2
AVAILABLE AT DISCIPLESHIPPROGRAM.ORG

GROUNDING YOUR FAITH

PSALM 8:4
What is man that you take thought of him, and the son of man that You care for him?

LIFE JACKET

The Greatness of Man
Imago Dei: (Lat. "image of God"). Refers to the fact that humanity carries a unique resemblance to God.

> " There are no ordinary people, it is immortals whom we joke with, work with, marry, snub, and exploit. – C.S. Lewis

> " If individuals live only seventy years, then a state, or a nation, or a civilization, which may last for a thousand years, is more important than an individual. But if Christianity is true, then the individual is not only more important but incomparably more important, for he is everlasting and the life of a state or a civilization, compared with his, is only a moment. – C.S. Lewis

THE FALL OF MAN

Is man a sinner because he sins or does he sin because he is a sinner?

ORIGINAL SIN

A broad term that refers to the effects that the first sin had on humanity or to the "origin" of sin.

IMPUTED SIN

Specifically refers to the guilt or condemnation of the first sin which was imputed to humanity.

INHERITED SIN

Specifically refers to the transferral of the sinful nature.

PERSONAL SIN

Specifically refers to the sins that are committed by individuals.

PELAGIANISM DEFINITION:

Man is inherently good. The Fall did not bring condemnation upon any but Adam. Man is born like Adam with the same ability to choose between good and evil. Man sins as a result of bad examples that began with Adam. Grace is available if necessary.

QUESTIONS:

Is man morally good? **Yes**

What is our relation to Adam? **He set a bad example**

Then why does man do bad? **Lots of bad examples**

Does man need the cross and grace? **No, but they are both available for the weak**

PERSONAL SIN

Which one of the life jacket illustrations would this be?

SEMI-PELAGIANISM

Definition: Man was affected by the fall, but not to the degree that he cannot make moves on his own toward God and cooperate with him in the salvation process.

QUESTIONS:

Is man morally good? **He is morally injured.**

What is our relation to Adam? **His sin caused us to be weak.**

Then why does man do bad? **Because we have a hurt nature.**

Does man need the cross and grace? **Yes, but we can contribute or cooperate with God to accomplish salvation.**

INHERITED CORRUPTION
PSALM 51:5

AUGUSTINIANISM

Definition: The Fall brought condemnation and guilt upon all men. Man is totally corrupted and inclined toward evil. Man has free will, but that will is governed by his sinful nature. Man sins, therefore, because he is a sinner.

QUESTIONS:

Is man morally good? **No, he is evil.**

What is our relation to Adam? **We are condemned in Adam and have inherited his sinful nature.**

Then why does man do bad? **Because we are born sinners.**

Does man need the cross and grace? **Yes. We contribute nothing to our salvation but sin.**

INPUTED SIN/GUILT ROMANS 5:12;18

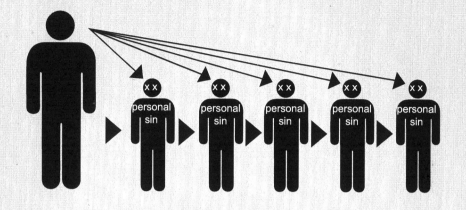

INHERITED CORRUPTION PSALM 51:5

> " Command whatever you want, but give whatever you command.
> - Augustine

ENEMIES/ALLIES

PELAGIUS

ca. AD 354 – ca. AD 420/440
Believed that man was born
without sin, having no relation to
Adam. Grace was only available if
needed. Condemned at the Second
Council of Orange in 529

AUGUSTINE

354 – 430
Believed that man was born condemned in Adam with no ability to
make a move toward God outside of
God's grace.

DIGGING INTO THE WORD

PSALM 8:4

What is man that you take thought of him, and the son of man that You care for him?

GENESIS 1:27

So God created man in his own image, in the image of God he created him; male and female he created them.

JAMES 3:8-9

But no one can tame the tongue; it is a restless evil and full of deadly poison. With it we bless our Lord and Father, and with it we curse men, who have been made in the likeness of God.

GENESIS 2:17

But from the tree of the knowledge of good and evil you shall not eat, for in the day that you eat from it you will surely die.

EPHESIANS 2:1-3

And you were dead in your trespasses and sins, in which you formerly walked according to the course of this world, according to the prince of the power of the air, of the spirit that is now working in the sons of disobedience. Among them we too all formerly lived in the lusts of our flesh, indulging the desires of the flesh and of the mind, and were by nature children of wrath, even as the rest.

JOHN 3:3

Jesus answered and said to him, 'Truly, truly, I say to you, unless one is born again he cannot see the kingdom of God.'

PSALM 51:5

Behold, I was brought forth in iniquity, and in sin did my mother conceive me.

ROMANS 5:19

For as through the one man's disobedience the many were made sinners, even so through the obedience of the One the many will be made righteous.

ROMANS 3:10-12

There is no one righteous, not even one; there is no one who understands, no one who seeks God. All have turned away, they have together become worthless; there is no one who does good, not even one.

ROMANS 5:19

For as through the one man's disobedience the many were made sinners, even so through the obedience of the One the many will be made righteous.

ROMANS 3:10-12

There is no one righteous, not even one; there is no one who understands, no one who seeks God. All have turned away, they have together become worthless; there is no one who does good, not even one.

How should the reality that man, believer and unbeliever alike, carries the imago dei affect the way we treat one another?

If man is truly dead with no ability to come to God on our own, how does that affect your view of salvation?

SESSION 3

TRINITY

ADDITIONAL RESOURCES FOR SESSION 3
AVAILABLE AT DISCIPLESHIPPROGRAM.ORG

PINE CONE

CONFESSION OF THE TRINITY

We believe in one God who is one in essence, yet three in person. All three members of the Trinity are eternally God, all of whom are equal.

THREE PRIMARY BELIEFS:

1. We believe the Bible teaches that God is the only God.

2. We believe the Bible teaches the Father is God, Jesus is God, and the Holy Spirit is God.

3. We believe the Bible teaches they are not each other.

The three major Christian traditions, Protestant, Roman Catholic, and Eastern Orthodox, which make up over 95% of professing Christians throughout history, have the same firm confession about the Trinity.

One of the hallmarks of a Christian "cult" is the denial of the Trinity.

Oneness Pentecostals

Jehovah's Witnesses

Mormons

Christadelphians

CHURCHES THAT BELIEVE IN THE TRINITY

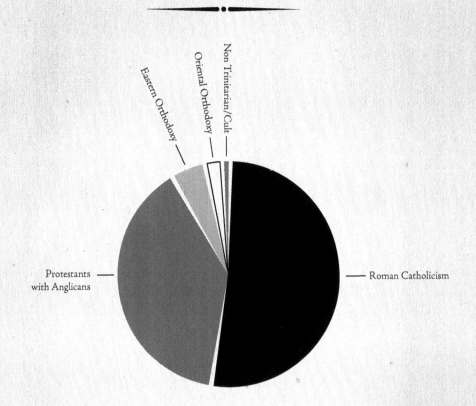

MAJOR CHRISTIAN TRADITIONS CHART

Is the doctrine of the Trinity a Contradiction?

Contradiction:
We believe in one God who is three Gods.

Not a Contradiction:
We believe in one God who is three persons.

Paradox, yes. Mysterious, yes. Contradiction, no.

SUBORDINATIONALISM

The belief that all three members of the Trinity are God, but that one or more are greater than the others.

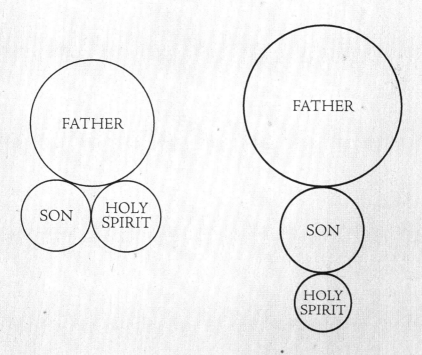

TRITHEISM

The belief that all three members of the Trinity are God, but that they are separate Gods, sharing in a similar nature.

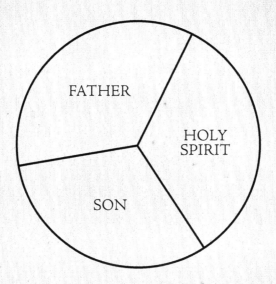

MODALISM

The belief that all three members of the Trinity are representative of one God who shows himself in three ways.

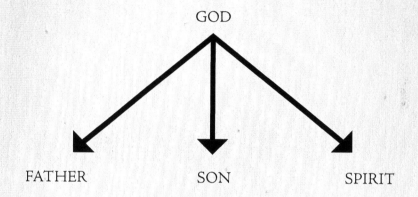

NICENE (CONSTANTINOPLE) CREED

We believe in one God, the Father, the Almighty [pantokratora], creator of all that is seen and unseen. We believe in one Lord, Jesus Christ, the only Son of God, eternally begotten [pro panton ton aionon] of the Father, God from God, Light from Light, true God from true God, begotten, not made, of the same essence [homoousion] with the Father.

Through him all things were made. For us and for our salvation he came down from heaven: by the power of the Holy Spirit he became incarnate from the Virgin Mary, and was made man. For our sake he was crucified under Pontius Pilate; he suffered death and was buried. On the third day he rose again in accordance with the Scriptures; he ascended into heaven and is seated at the right hand of the Father. He will come again in glory to judge the living and the dead, and his kingdom will have no end.

We believe in the Holy Spirit, the Lord, the giver of life, who proceeds from the Father. With the Father and the Son he is worshipped and glorified. He has spoken through the Prophets. We believe in one holy catholic and apostolic Church. We acknowledge one baptism for the forgiveness of sins. We look for the resurrection of the dead, and the life of the world to come. Amen.

WEEDS/PLANTS

ARIUS
AD 250 – 336

Believed that Christ was a created god who was like or similar to (homoiousia) the Father. Modern adherents: Jehovah's Witnesses Condemned at the Council of Nicea in 325

ATHANASIUS
c. 293 – 373

Believe that Christ was eternal and homoousia (of the same substance) as the Father

SABELLIUS
AD 215

Believed in one God who showed himself in three ways. Modern adherents: Oneness Pentecostals Condemned at the Council of Antioch in 286

CAPPADOCIAN FATHERS

(Basil the Great, Gregory of Nyssa, Gregory Nazianzus) 4th century Helped formulate our current articulation of the Trinity

--- • ---

DEUT. 6:4

Hear, O Israel: The Lord our God is one Lord.

ISAIAH 44:6

Thus says the Lord, the King of Israel and his Redeemer, the Lord of hosts: "I am the first and I am the last, and there is no God besides Me."

JOHN 1:1

In the beginning was the Word, and the Word was with God, and the Word was God.

2 PETER 1:1

To those who have received a faith of the same kind as ours, by the righteousness of our God and Savior, Jesus Christ.

COLOSSIANS 1:15-17a

He is the image of the invisible God, the firstborn of all creation. For by Him all things were created, both in the heavens and on earth, visible and invisible, whether thrones or dominions or rulers or authorities all things have been created through Him and for Him. He is before all things, and in Him all things hold together.

2 COR. 3:17–18

Now the Lord is the Spirit, and where the Spirit of the Lord is, there is liberty. But we all, with unveiled face, beholding as in a mirror the glory of the Lord, are being transformed into the same image from glory to glory, just as from the Lord, the Spirit.

ACTS 5:3–4

But Peter said, "Ananias, why has Satan filled your heart to lie to the Holy Spirit and to keep back some of the price of the land? While it remained unsold, did it not remain your own? And after it was sold, was it not under your control? Why is it that you have conceived this deed in your heart? You have not lied to men but to God."

MATTHEW 3:16-17

As soon as Jesus was baptized, he went up out of the water. At that moment heaven was opened, and he saw the Spirit of God descending like a dove and lighting on him. And a voice from heaven said, "This is my Son, whom I love; with him I am well pleased."

MATTHEW 28:19

Go therefore and make disciples of all the nations, baptizing them in the name of the Father and the Son and the Holy Spirit.

EPHESIANS 2:18

For through him we both have access to the Father by one Spirit.

GROWING DEEP

WHAT'S WRONG WITH THESE ILLUSTRATIONS?

- 3-in-1 Shampoo

- 3-leaf clover

- Egg

- Water

- One person is husband, son and father

BEST ILLUSTRATION:

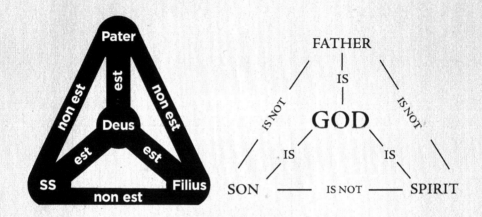

How would you explain your view of the Trinity before this lesson? (were you leaning toward subordinationalism, modalism, tritheism, etc.)

Has your view of the Trinity changed or grown? Please explain...

Why do you think God wants you to have a correct view of Himself?

ADDITIONAL RESOURCES FOR SESSION 3
AVAILABLE AT DISCIPLESHIPPROGRAM.ORG

S E S S I O N   4
J E S U S

ADDITIONAL RESOURCES FOR SESSION 4
AVAILABLE AT DISCIPLESHIPPROGRAM.ORG

APPLES & ORANGES

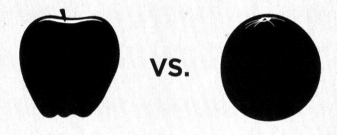

> " The greatest mystery in the Christian faith is that God became a man. - C.S. Lewis

The three major Christian traditions, Protestant, Roman Catholic, and Eastern Orthodox, which make up over 95% of professing Christians throughout history, have the same firm confession about the Christ's full humanity.

HYPOSTATIC UNION

In the incarnation, the second person of the Trinity became fully man while remaining fully God. Therefore, Christ was of two natures, yet one person.

	UNITY	DIVERSITY
TRINITY	NATURE	PERSONS
JESUS	PERSON	NATURES

How can an infinite God become a finite man?

GROWING DEEP

APOLLINARIANISM

Definition: Christ was God who took on a human body without a human mind/soul/spirit. The divine mind took the place of what would have been the immaterial part of man. The Word became flesh only in the sense that God took on a human body. As some have termed it, Christ was "God in a bod" or "God wearing a man-suit."

What is wrong with Apollinarianism?

NESTORIANISM

Definition: Christ was fully man and fully God, and these two natures were united in purpose, not person. Christ was two persons with two natures.

What is wrong with Nestorianism?

EUTYCHIANISM:

Definition: Christ's human nature was integrated with His divine nature, form-
ing a new nature. Christ was from two natures before the union, but only one
after the union.

What is wrong with Eutychianism?

> " What God has not assumed is not saved. - Gregory of Nazianzus

CHALCEDON CREED (451AD)

Therefore, following the holy fathers, we all with one accord teach men to acknowledge one and the same Son, our Lord Jesus Christ, at once complete in Godhead and complete in manhood, truly God and truly man, consisting also of a reasonable soul and body; of one substance with the Father as regards his Godhead, and at the same time of one substance with us as regards his manhood; like us in all respects, apart from sin; as regards his Godhead, begotten of the Father before the ages, but yet as regards his manhood begotten, for us men and for our salvation, of Mary the Virgin, the God-bearer one and the same Christ, Son, Lord, Only-begotten, recognized in two natures, without confusion, without change, without division, without separation; the distinction of natures being in no way annulled by the union, but rather the characteristics of each nature being preserved and coming together to form one person and subsistence, not as parted or separated into two persons, but one and the same Son and Only-begotten God the Word, Lord Jesus Christ; even as the prophets from earliest times spoke of him, and our Lord Jesus Christ himself taught us, and the creed of the fathers has handed down to us.

Christ is 100% God and 100% man

WEEDS / PLANTS

NESTORIUS
c. 386–c. 451

Thought to have taught Nestorianism, although many challenge whether he truly taught this heresy. Condemned at the Council of Chalcedon in 451

CYRIL OF ALEXANDRIA
c. 376 – 444

Fought against Nestorius, believing the term "Theotokos" (Bearer of God) should be used for Mary, the mother of Jesus, rather than "Christotokos" (Bearer of Christ).

APOLLINARIUS
Died 390

Believed that Christ had a human body, but lacked a human mind. Condemned at the First Council of Constantinople and the Council of Chalcedon in 451

LEO I (THE GREAT)
ca. 400 – 461

Helped articulate the nature of Christ during the Christological controversies. His tome sent to the members of the council of Chalcedon served as bedrock for the Definition of Chalcedon.

EUTYCHES
c. 380—c. 456

Believed that Christ was of two natures before the incarnation, but only one after. Condemned at the Council of Chalcedon in 451

JOHN 1:14

And the Word became flesh, and dwelt among us, and we saw His glory, glory as of the only begotten from the Father, full of grace and truth.

LUKE 1:34-35

Mary said to the angel, "How can this be, since I am a virgin?" The angel answered and said to her, "The Holy Spirit will come upon you, and the power of the Most High will overshadow you; and for that reason the holy Child shall be called the Son of God."

PHILIPPIANS 2:5-8

Have this attitude in yourselves which was also in Christ Jesus, who, although He existed in the form of God, did not regard equality with God a thing to be grasped, but emptied Himself, taking the form of a bond-servant, and being made in the likeness of men. Being found in appearance as a man, He humbled Himself by becoming obedient to the point of death, even death on a cross.

HEBREWS 2:17-18

Therefore, He had to be made like His brethren in all things, so that He might become a merciful and faithful high priest in things pertaining to God, to make propitiation for the sins of the people. For since He Himself was tempted in that which He has suffered, He is able to come to the aid of those who are tempted.

LUKE 2:52

And Jesus kept increasing in wisdom and stature, and in favor with God and men.

HEBREWS 2:14-15

Since then the children share in flesh and blood, He Himself likewise also partook of the same, that through death He might render powerless him who had the power of death, that is, the devil; and might deliver those who through fear of death were subject to slavery all their lives.

What struck you most about tonight?

Do you think Jesus ever got sick? If so, does that have implications for your relationship with him?

If Jesus was fully God, why did Jesus say he did not know the time of his coming? (Matt. 24:36)

Has your view of Jesus grown tonight? Would you have considered your views Eutychian, Apollinarian or Nestorian before tonight?

ADDITIONAL RESOURCES FOR SESSION 4
AVAILABLE AT DISCIPLESHIPPROGRAM.ORG

SESSION 5

FAITH

ADDITIONAL RESOURCES FOR SESSION 5
AVAILABLE AT DISCIPLESHIPPROGRAM.ORG

Catholics, Protestants, and Eastern Orthodox all believe faith is an essential component for salvation.

Protestants believe faith alone is all a person has to have to be restored to fellowship with God and inherit eternal life.

GROWING DEEP

What is faith?

THE CHAIR

OPTION 1:
The blind step into the dark unknown

THE DARK UNKNOWN

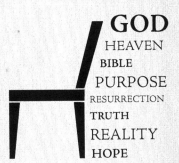

GOD
HEAVEN
BIBLE
PURPOSE
RESURRECTION
TRUTH
REALITY
HOPE

"The chair is right there. Trust me. Have a seat."

OPTION 2:
Step of faith despite the evidence.

IN SPITE OF THE EVIDENCE

EVIDENCE
PROOF
SCIENCE
LOGIC
INTELLECT

GOD
HEAVEN
BIBLE
PURPOSE
RESURRECTION
TRUTH
REALITY
HOPE

"The chair may not look like it can hold you, but it can.
Trust me. Have a seat."

OPTION 3:
A step of faith according to the evidence

───────•◦•───────

ACCORDING TO THE EVIDENCE

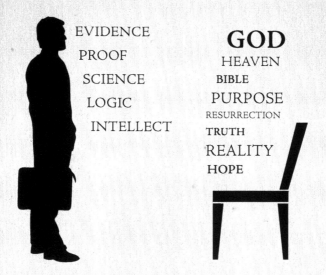

EVIDENCE
PROOF
SCIENCE
LOGIC
INTELLECT

GOD
HEAVEN
BIBLE
PURPOSE
RESURRECTION
TRUTH
REALITY
HOPE

"Examine the chair and see that it is trustworthy.
Then have a seat."

OPTION 4:
Christian Faith

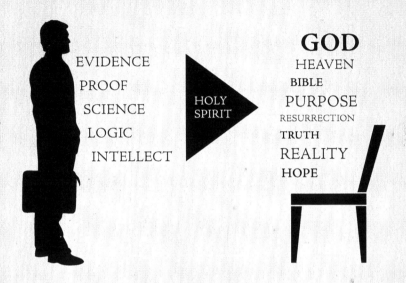

"Examine the chair and see that it is trustworthy.
Then have a seat."

THREE ASPECTS TO SAVING FAITH:

1: CONTENT (*notitia*)

2; CONVICTION (*assensus*)

3: TRUST (*fiducia*)

What does faith without content look like?

What does faith without conviction look like?

APOLOGETICS: Gk. apologia.

The task of Christians to intellectually defend their faith increasing their conviction that it is true.

What does faith without trust look like?

sola fide

sola fide: Lat. "faith alone" The Reformed Protestant principle that justification (being made right with God) is by faith alone in Christ alone. Works do not contribute in any way to our justification.

BIBLICAL MATHEMATICS:

works ≠ salvation

works + faith ≠ salvation

faith = salvation + works

> " Its faith alone that saves, but the faith that saves will not be alone.

HEB. 11:1

Now faith is the assurance of things hoped for, the conviction of things not seen.

EPH. 2:8-9

For by grace you have been saved through faith. And this is not your own doing; it is the gift of God, not a result of works, so that no one may boast.

1 COR. 2:14-15

The unbeliever does not receive the things of the Spirit of God, for they are foolishness to him. And he cannot understand them, because they are spiritually discerned. The one who is spiritual discerns all things, yet he himself is understood by no one.

ROM. 3:21-22

But now the righteousness of God has been manifested apart from the law, although the Law and the Prophets bear witness to it--the righteousness of God through faith in Jesus Christ for all who believe. For there is no distinction.

COFFEE TALK

‣ Why do you think it is so hard for us to rely completely on Christ? Why do we so often attempt to add to the work of Christ through our own efforts?

‣ In our society today, which element of faith do you believe is lacking the most: content, conviction, trust?

‣ In your life, what do you find lacking the most: content, conviction, trust? What can you do to change that?

ADDITIONAL RESOURCES FOR SESSION 5
AVAILABLE AT DISCIPLESHIPPROGRAM.ORG

DISCIPLESHIP PROGRAM

SESSION 6

LIVING

WITH

GOD

ADDITIONAL RESOURCES FOR SESSION 6
AVAILABLE AT DISCIPLESHIPPROGRAM.ORG

GROUNDING YOUR FAITH

* Ninety percent of Americans say they pray every day.

* Many people pray as a daily routine.

* Some people have routine prayers that they say before dinner or before bed.

* Prayer itself is a universal human phenomenon which is a vital part and sign of our need to worship.

What is Prayer?

God wants to talk with us; we were created for a relationship with him.

> ❝ Nothing feels more right, more like what we are created to be and to do. Yet at the same time we are confronted with great mysteries. Who hasn't struggled with the puzzle of unanswered prayer? Who hasn't wondered how a finite person can commune with the infinite Creator of the universe? Who hasn't questioned whether prayer isn't merely psychological manipulation after all? We do our best, of course, to answer these knotty questions but when all is said and done, there is a sense in which these mysteries remain unanswered andunanswerable . . . At such times we must learn to become comfortable with the mystery. -Richard Foster

LORD'S PRAYER (Disciples' Prayer):
Matt. 6:9-13; Luke 11:2-4

KING JAMES VERSION
"Our Father which art in heaven, Hallowed be thy name. Thy kingdom come.
Thy will be done in earth, as it is in heaven. Give us this day our daily bread.
And forgive us our debts, as we forgive our debtors. And lead us not into
temptation, but deliver us from evil. (KJV)

NEW LIVING TRANSLATION
"Our Father in heaven, may your name be kept holy. May your Kingdom
come soon. May your will be done on earth, as it is in heaven. Give us today
the food we need, and forgive us our sins, as we have forgiven those who sin
against us. And don't let us yield to temptation, but rescue us from the evil
one. (NLT)

1. PRAYER AS WORSHIP

"Our Father in heaven, may your name be holy."

2. PRAYER AS RECOGNITION OF GOD'S WILL

"May your Kingdom come soon. May your will be done on earth, as it is
in heaven."

3. PRAYER AS AN EXPRESSION OF DEPENDENCE
"Give us this day our daily bread."

4. PRAYER AS CONFESSION
"Forgive us our sins as we forgive those who sin against us."

5. PRAYER AS A CALL FOR DELIVERANCE IN WARFARE

"And don't let us yield to temptation, but rescue us from the evil one."

6. PRAYER AS INTERCESSION

"Give us this day our daily bread."

"Forgive us our sins as we forgive those who sin against us."

"And don't let us yield to temptation, but rescue us from the evil one."

PRAYER AS AN ARGUMENT MADE TO GOD

• Jacob wrestled an Angel (Gen, 22:34)

• Moses turned the hand of God (Ex. 32:11-14)

• Abraham and Sodom (Gen. 18:23-32)

Why does God seem to want us to make an argument in prayer?

PRAYER LOGISTICS #1:
When is the best time to pray?

PRAYER LOGISTICS #2:
Where is the best place to pray?

PSALM 139:7-10

Where can I go from Your Spirit? Or where can I flee from Your presence? If I ascend to heaven, You are there; If I make my bed in Sheol, behold, You are there. If I take the wings of the dawn, if I dwell in the remotest part of the sea, even there Your hand will lead me, And Your right hand will lay hold of me.

JOHN. 4:20-24

[Woman at the well speaking] "Our fathers worshiped in this mountain, and you people say that in Jerusalem is the place where men ought to worship." Jesus said to her, "Woman, believe Me, an hour is coming when neither in this mountain nor in Jerusalem will you worship the Father. You worship what you do not know; we worship what we know, for salvation is from the Jews. But an hour is coming, and now is, when the true worshipers will worship the Father in spirit and truth; for such people the Father seeks to be His worshipers. God is spirit, and those who worship Him must worship in spirit and truth."

PRAYER LOGISTICS #3:
Who do we pray to?

To the Father

Through the Son

By the Spirit

PRAYER METHODS:

1. Devotional

2. Situational

3. Conversational

TRANSCENDENTAL MEDITATION
vs. PRAYER

NOWHERE   GOD

                        ▲

ANXIETY   ANXIETY

MEDITATION   PRAYER

PHIL. 4:6

Do not be anxious about anything, but in everything by prayer and supplication with thanksgiving let your requests be made known to God.

WHAT PRAYER IS NOT:

• Rabbit's foot/genie in a bottle

• Request to granddad

• A pithy rote call to God

MATT. 6:7

And when you are praying, do not use meaningless repetition as the Gentiles do, for they suppose that they will be heard for their many words.

"In Jesus' Name"...a magic formula?

JOHN 14:14

If you ask Me anything in My name, I will do it.

What does "in Jesus' name" mean?

JOHN 5:43

I have come in My Father's name, and you do not receive Me; if another comes in his own name, you will receive him.

To pray "in Jesus' name" means that we are praying according to the will of Christ, as his representative.

HEB. 4:16

Let us then with confidence draw near to the throne of grace, that we may receive mercy and find grace to help in time of need.

MARK 9:29

And he said to them, "This kind cannot be driven out by anything but prayer."

ROM. 8:26

Likewise the Spirit helps us in our weakness. For we do not know what to pray for as we ought, but the Spirit himself intercedes for us with groanings too deep for words.

JOHN 15:7

If you abide in me, and my words abide in you, ask whatever you wish, and it will be done for you.

LUKE 6:12

In these days he went out to the mountain to pray, and all night he continued in prayer to God.

LUKE 18:1

And he told them a parable to the effect that they ought always to pray and not lose heart.

PHIL. 4:6-7

Do not be anxious about anything, but in everything by prayer and supplication with thanksgiving let your requests be made known to God. And the peace of God, which surpasses all understanding, will guard your hearts and minds in Christ Jesus.

1 THESS 5:17

Pray without ceasing.

- What are some frustrations you have with your prayer life?

- Share a time when God definitely answered a prayer.

- What is an argument that you might be able to put to God about some current issue in your life? Express it like Moses did.

- Name a deficiency in your prayer life. Have your group offer suggestions to help you.

ADDITIONAL RESOURCES FOR SESSION 6
AVAILABLE AT DISCIPLESHIPPROGRAM.ORG

SESSION 7

LIVING

WITH

GOD'S WORD

ADDITIONAL RESOURCES FOR SESSION 7
AVAILABLE AT DISCIPLESHIPPROGRAM.ORG

BASIC BIBLE STATISTICS

+ The Bible is without qualification the bestselling book of all time.

+ 92% percent of Americans own at least one Bible.

+ 37% say they read the Bible at least once a week.

+ 14% say that they study the Bible each week.

+ 14% percent say that they are involved in a Bible study group.

BIBLE KNOWLEDGE STATISTICS

+ 50% of adults interviewed nationwide could name any of the four Gospels of the New Testament.

+ Just 37% of those interviewed could name all four Gospels.

+ Only 42% of adults were able to name five of the Ten Commandments correctly.

+ Just 70% were able to name the town where Jesus was born.

+ Just 42% could identify him as the person who delivered the Sermon on the Mount.

BIBLE KNOWLEDGE STATISTICS

+ 38% of Americans believe that both the Old and New Testaments were written several decades after Jesus' death and resurrection (While this is true of the New Testament, the entire Old Testament was written hundreds of years before the birth of Jesus Christ).

+ 12% of adults believe that Noah's wife was Joan of Arc.

+ 49% believe that the Bible teaches that money is the root of all evil. (The love of money is said to be a root of all types of evil).

+ 75% believe that the Bible teaches that God helps those who help themselves.

SOME COMMON BIBLE STUDY METHODS:

+ Lucky lotto: (eyes closed) – "I will read this verse"

+ Brussels Sprout: "Do I have to?"

+ Channel Changer: "Let's read something else"

+ Concord: "Watch how fast I can finish"

+ Baseball card: "I'm very picky"

+ Clint Eastwood: "I don't need anyone's help"

+ Magical: "Abracadabra ... It applies to my life"

+ Indiana Jones: "Let's find the hidden meaning"

KEY TERMS

INTERPRETATION:

The process by which the Scriptures are understood by the reader.

HERMENEUTICS:

The theory, method, or rules of biblical interpretation.

EXEGESIS:

Gk. ex, "out" + hēgeisthai, "to lead." The process of discovering the original meaning of the biblical text by studying the text according to the authorial intent in its historical contexts.

TIMELESS AUDIENCE	
TIME BOUND AUDIENCE	
ANCIENT AUDIENCE	CONTEMPORARY AUDIENCE

2: "WHAT DOES IT MEAN FOR ALL
PEOPLE OF ALL TIMES?"

TIMELESS AUDIENCE

TIME BOUND AUDIENCE

1. WHAT DID IT
MEAN THEN?

ANCIENT AUDIENCE

3. HOW DOES IT
APPLY TODAY?

CONTEMPORARY
AUDIENCE

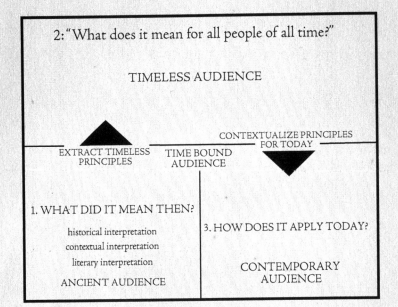

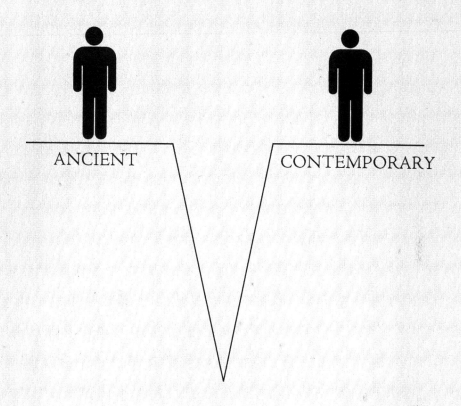

ANCIENT   CONTEMPORARY

HISTORY/CULTURE

+ **Author:** Who wrote the book?

+ **Audience:** Who was it written to?

+ **Occasion:** Why was it written?

+ **Time:** When was it written?

+ **Place or origin:** Where was it written from?

+ **Destination:** Where was it written to?

+ **Attitude:** What was the attitude of the author when he wrote?

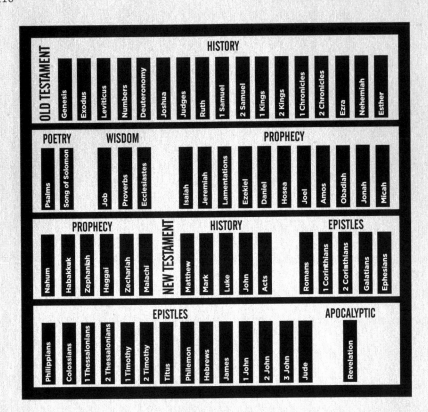

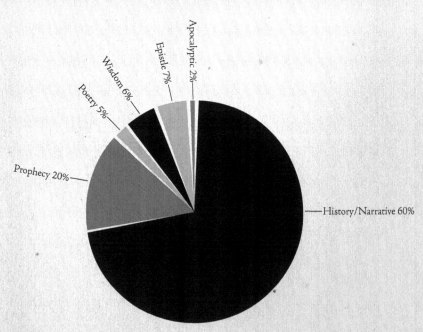

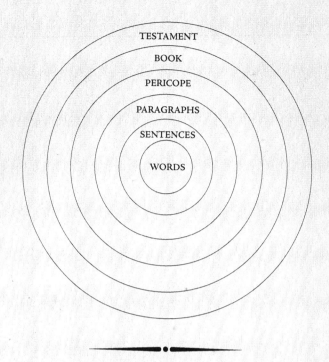

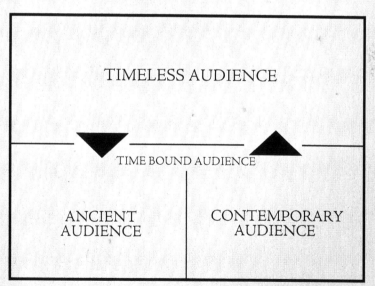

PRACTICAL EISEGESIS:

Gk. *eis*, "in" + *hēgeisthai*, "to lead."

The process of conforming your beliefs and the Scripture to your daily life and needs.

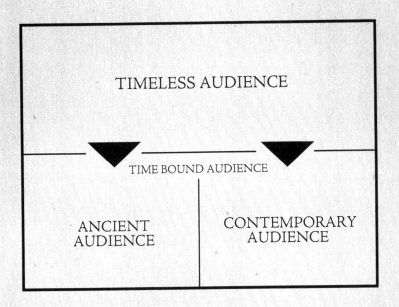

THEOLOGICAL EISEGESIS:

Gk. *eis*, "in" + *hēgeisthai*, "to lead." The process of conforming the Scripture to your presupposed system of belief.

ARCHAIC APPLICATION FALLACY:

The process of directly applying Scripture without extracting the timeless principles.

DIGGING INTO THE WORD

2 TIM. 3:14-17

You, however, continue in the things you have learned and become convinced of, knowing from whom you have learned them, and that from childhood you have known the sacred writings which are able to give you the wisdom that leads to salvation through faith which is in Christ Jesus. All Scripture is inspired by God and profitable for teaching, for reproof, for correction, for training in righteousness; so that the man of God may be adequate, equipped for every good work.

2 TIM. 2:15

Be diligent to present yourself approved to God as a workman who does not need to be ashamed, handling accurately the word of truth.

JOSH. 1:8

This book of the law shall not depart from your mouth, but you shall meditate on it day and night, so that you may be careful to do according to all that is written in it; for then you will make your way prosperous, and then you will have success.

PSA. 119:12-16

Blessed are you, O LORD; teach me your statutes! With my lips I declare all the rules of your mouth. In the way of your testimonies I delight as much as in all riches. I will meditate on your precepts and fix my eyes on your ways. 16 I will delight in your statutes; I will not forget your word.

2 TIM. 4:2

Preach the word; be ready in season and out of season; reprove, rebuke, exhort, with great patience and instruction.

COFFEE TALK

READ MATT. 18:20

+ How do you think people have traditionally understood this passage?

+ Find the context of the passage in your Bible. Where does the section that this verse occurs in begin? (Hint: Read a few verses up)

+ Read the entire section.

+ What is the subject of this section (i.e. what is this section talking about)?

+ Considering the subject of the section, what does it mean to have 2 or 3 gathered in Christ's name in this context? (Hint: read verse 16 again).

READ REV. 3:20

◆ How do you think people have traditionally understood this passage?

◆ Find the context of the passage. Who is Christ talking to? Is it those in the church or non-churched people?

◆ Since this passage is talking to believers, what are the implications? Is this a salvation invitation?

◆ The passage says "I will come in to him" not "I will come into him." What is the difference?

◆ How does this relate to the idea that unbelievers are supposed to ask Christ into their heart? Does this passage teach this?

ADDITIONAL RESOURCES FOR SESSION 7
AVAILABLE AT DISCIPLESHIPPROGRAM.ORG

SESSION 8

LIVING

WITH

GOD'S PEOPLE

ADDITIONAL RESOURCES FOR SESSION 8
AVAILABLE AT DISCIPLESHIPPROGRAM.ORG

GROUNDING YOUR FAITH

• Forty percent of Americans say they attend church weekly.

• There are three major Christian Traditions:

– Roman Catholic

– Protestant

– Eastern Orthodox

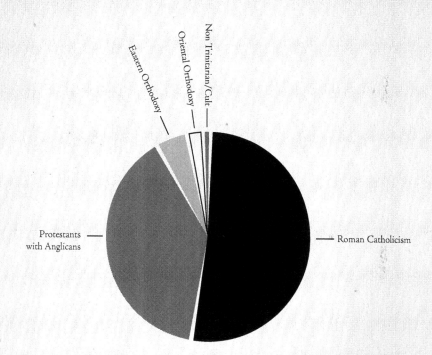

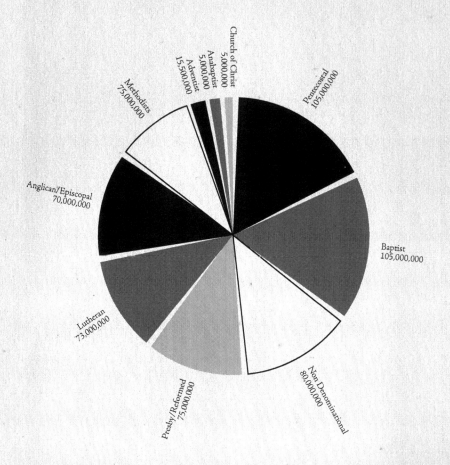

+ There are an estimated 3.7 million Christian churches, but this does not
  include house churches.

+ There are close to 50,000 churches started every year.

+ The largest church in America has 43,000 people.

+ The largest church in the world is in Korea and it boasts a
  membership of 830,000.

WHAT IS CHURCH?

CHURCH VISIBLE
- The local expression of the universal Body of Christ.

CHURCH INVISIBLE
- The Body of Christ made up of all those who have trusted in Christ since the day of Pentecost.

GROWING DEEP

HEBREWS 10:25

Not forsaking our own assembling together, as is the habit of some,
but encouraging one another; and all the more as you see the day drawing near.

What happens to a log when it is taken away from a fire?

What does a person lose without community?

List at least five things:

1.

2.

3.

4.

5.

"It is not good that man should be alone." -God (Gen. 2:18)

"Let us make man in our image." -God (Gen. 1:26)

Church is not just something that you go to.

Church is not a building.

Church is not a denomination.

Church is something you are and do.

FELLOWSHIP

ORDINANCES   DISCIPLINE

COMMUNITY

ACCOUNTABILITY   ENCOURAGEMENT

SPIRITUAL GIFTS

BUT THE FRUIT OF THE SPIRIT IS:

1. Love

2. Joy

3. Peace

4. Patience

5. Kindness

6. Goodness

7. Faithfulness

8. Gentleness

9. Self-control

WHICH OF THESE WOULD YOU LOSE IF YOU DID NOT HAVE COMMUNITY?

+ Love one another. (Rom. 12:10)

+ Outdo one another in showing honor. (Rom. 12:10)

+ Be of the same mind with one another. (Rom. 12:16)

+ Let us not judge one another. (Rom. 14:13)

+ Build up one another. (Rom. 14:19)

+ Accept one another. (Rom. 15:17)

+ Instruct one another. (Rom. 15:14)

+ Serve one another. (Gal. 5:13)

- Put up with one another. (Eph. 4:2)

- Forgive one another (Eph. 4:32)

- Be subject to one another. (Eph. 5:21)

- Think one another more significant than yourself. (Phil. 2:3)

- Do not lie to one another. (Col. 3:9)

- Admonish one another. (Col. 3:16)

- Comfort one another. (1 Thess. 4:18)

- Encourage one another. (1 Thess. 5:11)

- Live in peace with one another. (1 Thess. 5:13)

• Stimulate one another to love. (Heb. 10:24)

• Pray for one another. (Jam. 5:16)

• Confess your sins to one another. (Jam. 5:16)

• Be hospitable to one another. (1Pet 4:9)

• Serve one another. (1Pet 4:10)

• Have fellowship with one another. (1John 1:7)

There are over 50 direct "one another" commands in the New Testament.

WRONG ATTITUDES TOWARD CHURCH:

♦ Nomadic Christian

♦ Exclusive Christian

♦ Inclusive Christian

♦ Burned Christian

♦ Consumer Christian

♦ Online Christian

DIGGING INTO THE WORD

HEBREWS 10:25

Not forsaking our own assembling together, as is the habit of some, but encouraging one another; and all the more as you see the day drawing near.

ACTS 2:41-47

So those who received his word were baptized, and there were added that day about three thousand souls. And they devoted themselves to the apostles' teaching and the fellowship, to the breaking of bread and the prayers. And awe came upon every soul, and many wonders and signs were being done through the apostles. And all who believed were together and had all things in common. And they were selling their possessions and belongings and distributing the proceeds to all, as any had need. And day by day, attending the temple together and breaking bread in their homes, they received their food with glad and generous hearts, praising God and having favor with all the people. And the Lord added to their number day by day those who were being saved.

HEB. 13:17

"Obey your leaders and submit to them, for they are keeping watch over your souls, as those who will have to give an account. Let them do this with joy and not with groaning, for that would be of no advantage to you."

1 COR. 11:26

For as often as you eat this bread and drink the cup, you proclaim the Lord's death until he comes.

1 COR. 12:7

But to each one is given the manifestation of the Spirit for the common good.

1 COR. 12:12-18

For even as the body is one and yet has many members, and all the members of the body, though they are many, are one body, so also is Christ. For by one Spirit we were all baptized into one body, whether Jews or Greeks, whether slaves or free, and we were all made to drink of one Spirit. For the body is not one member, but many. If the foot says, "Because I am not a hand, I am not a part of the body," it is not for this reason any the less a part of the body. And if the ear says, "Because I am not an eye, I am not a part of the body," it is not for this reason any the less a part of the body. If the whole body were an eye, where would the hearing be? If the whole were hearing, where would the sense of smell be? But now God has placed the members, each one of them, in the body, just as He desired.

EPH. 4:32

Be kind to one another, tender-hearted, forgiving each other, just as God in Christ also has forgiven you.

LUKE 18:1

And he told them a parable to the effect that they ought always to pray and not lose heart.

GEN 2:18

Then the LORD God said, "It is not good for the man to be alone; I will make him a helper suitable for him."

- It was said during the session that church is not simply a place to go, but something that you do. List some ways we can "do" church every day.

- What are some ways that we often neglect the gathering together of believers?

- Do you sometimes neglect Christian fellowship? Why?

- Why is it important that you "belong" to a local body of believers?

ADDITIONAL RESOURCES FOR SESSION 8
AVAILABLE AT DISCIPLESHIPPROGRAM.ORG

SESSION 9

LIVING
WITH
PAIN
AND
SUFFERING

ADDITIONAL RESOURCES FOR SESSION 9
AVAILABLE AT DISCIPLESHIPPROGRAM.ORG

- 200 million Christians in at least 60 countries are denied fundamental human rights solely because of their faith.

- 176,000 Christians are martyred each year.

- If the trend continues, 210,000 Christians will be martyred in 2025.

- Abel was the first Christian martyr in the Bible (Gen. 4:8).

- James was the last Christian martyr in the Bible (Acts 12:2).

- The divorce rate among Christians and non-Christians is about the same.

• The percentage of Christian who get cancer is the same as the percentage of non-Christians.

• The death rate of Christians and non-Christians is the same:

• 1/1 Christians who tithe die.

• 1/1 Christians who pray regularly die

• 1/1 Christians who go to church regularly die

• 1/1 Christians die

• 1/1 non-Christians die

QUESTION FROM A NON-CHRISTIAN:

"...I suppose the faithful think they'll get their just rewards, and we'll get our just punishment, in the next life, but it sure doesn't look like they're getting any special payoff in this life. So why do believers just keep talking about miracles, blessing and wonders ALL THE TIME, when there is absolutely NO evidence for any of these things... Is there any evidence to show that Christians that pray to their god for better protection from harm are better protected than we the infidels?."

DEATH OF THE 12 APOSTLES

1. **James** - Killed with a sword. 45 A.D.

2. **Peter** - Hung on a cross "head down." A.D. 64

3. **Andrew** - Hung from an olive tree. A.D. 70

4. **Thomas** - Burned alive. A.D. 70

5. **Phillip** - Crucified. A.D. 54

6. **Matthew** - Beheaded. A.D. 65

7. **Nathanael** - Crucified. A.D. 70

8. **James** - Thrown from the temple. A.D. 63

9. **Simon** - Crucified. A.D. 74

10. **Judas Thaddeus** - Beaten with sticks. A.D. 72

11. **Matthias** - Stoned on a cross. A.D. 70

12. **John** - Natural death. A.D. 95

13. **Paul** - Beheaded. A.D. 69

GROWING DEEP

THE PROBLEM OF SUFFERING AND EVIL DEFINED:

Premise 1:

God is all-good (omnibenevolent)

Premise 2:

God is all powerful (omnipotent)

Premise 3:

Suffering and evil exist

Conclusion: An all-good all-powerful God could not exist since there is so much suffering and evil in the world. If he did, he would eradicate it.

WRONG WAYS TO UNDERSTAND SUFFERING AND EVIL:

The Sadotheistic Response:

Premise 1:
~~God is all-good (omnibenevolent)~~

Premise 2:
God is all powerful (omnipotent)

Premise 3:
Suffering and evil exist

Conclusion:
God does not really care whether suffering and evil occur.

WRONG WAYS TO UNDERSTAND SUFFERING AND EVIL:

Open Theistic Response:

Premise 1:
God is all-good (omnibenevolent)

~~Premise 2:~~
~~God is all powerful (omnipotent)~~

Premise 3:
Suffering and evil exist

Conclusion:
God has self-limited his abilities so that he can truly relate to mankind.
Therefore God cannot stop all suffering and evil.

WRONG WAYS TO UNDERSTAND SUFFERING AND EVIL:

The Pantheistic Response:

Premise 1:
God is all-good (omnibenevolent)

Premise 2:
God is all powerful (omnipotent)

~~**Premise 3:**~~
~~Suffering and evil exist~~

Conclusion:
Suffering and evil is are illusions that we create with our own mind. To eradicate them, we must deny their existence.

THE RIGHT WAY TO UNDERSTAND SUFFERING AND EVIL:

The Christian Response:

Premise 1:
God is all-good (omnibenevolent)

Premise 2:
God is all powerful (omnipotent)

Premise 3:
Suffering and evil exist

Conclusion:
God has a reason for allowing suffering and evil to accomplish a greater good, even if we never know what that reason is.

GEN. 50:20 "As for you, you meant evil against me, but God meant it for good in order to bring about this present result, to preserve many people alive."

The Christian faith is not based on an assumption of the absence of suffering, evil, and pain.

TYPES OF SUFFERING AND EVIL CHRISTIANS CAN EXPECT:

– **Physical:** pain, cancer, accidents, etc.

– **Emotional:** depression, anxiety, etc.

– **Financial:** bankruptcy, poverty, etc.

– **Spiritual:** sin, God's hiddenness and silence, etc.

– **Meaningless:** stubbing my toe, minor irritations.

– **Referred:** suffering of others.

WRONG VIEW #1:
Suffering is all Satan's fault.

JOB 1:6-12

"Now there was a day when the sons of God came to present themselves before the LORD, and Satan also came among them. And the LORD said to Satan, "From where do you come?" Then Satan answered the LORD and said, "From roaming about on the earth and walking around on it." And the LORD said to Satan, "Have you considered My servant Job? For there is no one like him on the earth, a blameless and upright man, fearing God and turning away from evil.

"Then Satan answered the LORD, "Does Job fear God for nothing? "Hast Thou not made a hedge about him and his house and all that he has, on every side? Thou hast blessed the work of his hands, and his possessions have increased in the land. "But put forth Thy hand now and touch all that he has; he will surely curse Thee to Thy face."

Then the LORD said to Satan, "Behold, all that he has is in your power, only do not put forth your hand on him." So Satan departed from the presence of the LORD.

Christian Response to Wrong View #1:

Satan does not rival God in power. Everything that he does has to be approved of God. God uses Satan to accomplish his perfect end.

WRONG VIEW #2:

Many Bible passages say that if we are to follow the Lord, we will be protected from suffering and prosper financially.

DEUT. 8:18

"But you shall remember the Lord your God, for it is He who is giving you power to make wealth, that He may confirm His covenant which He swore to your fathers, as it is this day."

> " I am fully convinced - I would die saying it is so - that it is the plan of Our Father God, in His great love and in His great mercy, that no believer should ever be sick; that every believer should live his full life span down here on this earth; and that every believer should finally just fall asleep in Jesus" (Kenneth E. Hagin, Seven Things You Should Know about Divine Healing, p. 21).

Christian Response to Wrong View #2:
There were certain promises made to theocratic Israel under the Old Covenant that do not apply to us today.

WRONG VIEW #3:

While the Lord will cause us to suffer, he will always restore us after a short time.

JOEL 2:25
"I will repay you for the years the locusts have eaten—the great locust and the young locust."

JOB   VS.   LAZARUS
BOOK
OF
JOB

LUKE
16:19-31

Christian Response to Wrong View #3:

While the Lord does often restore his people after a short time, sometimes the suffering of his people does not end until death.

WRONG VIEW #4:

Christians who suffer the most are the "best" Christians.

JOHN 21:21-23
"Peter therefore seeing him said to Jesus, "Lord, and what about this man?"
Jesus said to him, "If I want him to remain until I come, what is that to you?
You follow Me!" This saying therefore went out among the brethren that that
disciple would not die; yet Jesus did not say to him that he would not die, but
only, "If I want him to remain until I come, what is that to you?"

Christian Response to Wrong View #4:
While all Christians can expect some degree of suffering, suffering itself is not
an indication of God's love or lack thereof.

DIGGING INTO THE WORD

ACTS 9:16

I will show him how much he must suffer for my name.

ROM. 8:17-18

Now if we are children, then we are heirs--heirs of God and co-heirs with
Christ, if indeed we share in his sufferings in order that we may also share in
his glory. For I consider that our present sufferings are not worth comparing
with the glory that will be revealed in us.

ROM. 8:23

Not only so, but we ourselves, who have the firstfruits of the Spirit, groan
inwardly as we wait eagerly for our adoption as sons, the redemption of
our bodies.

2 COR. 1:7

And our hope for you is firm, because we know that just as you share in our sufferings, so also you share in our comfort.

2 COR. 4:16-18

Therefore we do not lose heart. Though outwardly we are wasting away, yet inwardly we are being renewed day by day. For our light and momentary troubles are achieving for us an eternal glory that far outweighs them all. So we fix our eyes not on what is seen, but on what is unseen. For what is seen is temporary, but what is unseen is eternal.

LUKE 18:1

And he told them a parable to the effect that they ought always to pray and not lose heart.

1 PET. 4:12-13

Beloved, do not be surprised at the fiery trial when it comes upon you to test you, as though something strange were happening to you. But rejoice insofar as you share Christ's sufferings, that you may also rejoice and be glad when his glory is revealed.

PHIL. 1:29

For it has been granted to you on behalf of Christ not only to believe on him, but also to suffer for him.

2 COR. 4:8-11

We are afflicted in every way, but not crushed; perplexed, but not driven to despair; persecuted, but not forsaken; struck down, but not destroyed; always carrying in the body the death of Jesus, so that the life of Jesus may also be manifested in our bodies. For we who live are always being given over to death for Jesus' sake, so that the life of Jesus also may be manifested in our mortal flesh.

1 PET. 2:20

For what credit is there if, when you sin and are harshly treated, you endure it with patience? But if when you do what is right and suffer for it you patiently endure it, this finds favor with God.

In what ways do you suffer right now? Be specific.

In what ways have you experienced "meaningless suffering"?

In what ways have you experienced "meaningful suffering"?

Knowing that God has destined us to some suffering with Christ, does this make you less desirous to be a Christian? Why or why not?

ADDITIONAL RESOURCES FOR SESSION 9
AVAILABLE AT DISCIPLESHIPPROGRAM.ORG

WEEK 10

LIVING
AS
LIGHTS

ADDITIONAL RESOURCES FOR SESSION 10
AVAILABLE AT DISCIPLESHIPPROGRAM.ORG

GROUNDING YOUR FAITH

+ God has no grandchildren.

+ Every person becomes a follower of Christ through another person.

+ Part of being a disciple is helping other people become disciples.

+ We need to be people who help lead people to Jesus.

MATTHEW 28:16-20

Now the eleven disciples went to Galilee, to the mountain to which Jesus had directed them. And when they saw him they worshiped him, but some doubted. And Jesus came and said to them, "All authority in heaven and on earth has been given to me. Go therefore and make disciples of all nations, baptizing them in the name of the Father and of the Son and of the Holy Spirit, teaching them to observe all that I have commanded you. And behold, I am with you always, to the end of the age."

+ We are God's Plan A to bring people to Himself. He has no Plan B.

ROMANS 10:14-15

How then will they call on him in whom they have not believed? And how are they to believe in him of whom they have never heard? And how are they to hear without someone preaching? And how are they to preach unless they are sent? As it is written, "How beautiful are the feet of those who preach the good news!"

ACTS 10

GROWING DEEP

REASONS WHY I DON'T LEAD PEOPLE TO JESUS:

1. I'm an introvert.

2. Public speaking is my biggest fear.

3. I don't know what to share.

4. I've tried and always been rejected.

5. They'll ask me a question I don't know how to answer.

6. I'm too bad of a person.

7. Someone else will do it.

8. All my friends are Christians.

9. My life, not my words, shares Jesus with others.

RELATIONAL VS. CONFRONTATIONAL METHODS:

Relational
Share with people about Jesus only after spending time developing a relationship (co-worker, friend, classmate, and neighbor)

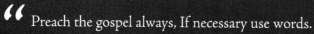

> " Preach the gospel always, If necessary use words.
> - St. Francis of Assisi.

Very popular mindset in the church today.

People point to Jesus as a "friend to sinners."

Confrontational

Asking someone to trust Jesus before developing a relationship with them.

- Mainly includes sharing with a stranger or someone we just barely know about Jesus.

1 PETER 3:15

In your hearts honor Christ the Lord as holy, always being prepared to make a defense to anyone who asks you for a reason for the hope that is in you.

We see this as a the prominent New Testament model (most used by Jesus, Paul and Peter)

A growing disciple of Christ should be prepared to use both methods:

Requires:

- Courage

- If the same person was dying of cancer and you knew the doctor to send them to, you would do it.

- Satan is trying to stop you; that's why it's so hard.

LUKE 9:26-27

"For whoever is ashamed of me and of my words, of him will the Son of Man be ashamed when he comes in his glory and the glory of the Father and of the holy angels. But I tell you truly, there are some standing here who will not taste death until they see the kingdom of God."

- A certain level of knowledge

- We all need to be growing in Apologetics
  - **Apologetics Program**
  - **The Theology Program**

- Restraint to keep the message of Jesus central
- People do not need to become Republicans to trust Jesus as their Savior
- People do not need to have the same views on the End Times to trust Jesus as their Savior

MAIN COMPONENTS WHEN SHARING THE GOSPEL:

1. Who needs salvation?

2. Why we need salvation?

3. How God provides salvation.

4. How we receive salvation.

5. The results of salvation.

1. WHO NEEDS SALVATION?

a. Everyone Needs Salvation

ROMANS 3:10-12; 23

As the Scriptures say, "No one is righteous—not even one. No one is truly wise; no one is seeking God. All have turned away; all have become useless. No one does good, not a single one." ... For everyone has sinned; we all fall short of God's glorious standard.

2. WHY WE NEED SALVATION?

a. The price (or consequence) of sin is death.

ROMANS 6:23

For the wages of sin is death, but the free gift of God is eternal life through Christ Jesus our Lord.

3. HOW GOD PROVIDES SALVATION.

a. Jesus Christ died for our sins. He paid the price for our death.

ROMANS 5:8

But God showed his great love for us by sending Christ to die for us while we were still sinners.

4. HOW WE RECEIVE SALVATION.

a. We receive salvation and eternal life through faith in Jesus Christ.

ROMANS 10:9-10; 13

If you confess with your mouth that Jesus is Lord and believe in your heart
that God raised him from the dead, you will be saved. For it is by believing
in your heart that you are made right with God, and it is by confessing with
your mouth that you are saved ... For "Everyone who calls on the name of the
Lord will be saved."

5. THE RESULTS OF SALVATION.

**a. Salvation through Jesus Christ brings us into a relationship of peace
with God.**

ROMANS 5:1

Therefore, since we have been made right in God's sight by faith, we have
peace with God because of what Jesus Christ our Lord has done for us.

ROMANS 8:1

So now there is no condemnation for those who belong to Christ Jesus.

ROMANS 8:38-39

And I am convinced that nothing can ever separate us from God's love.
Neither death nor life, neither angels nor demons, neither our fears for today
nor our worries about tomorrow—not even the powers of hell can separate
us from God's love. No power in the sky above or in the earth below—
indeed, nothing in all creation will ever be able to separate us from the love of
God that is revealed in Christ Jesus our Lord.

RESPONDING:

1. Admit you are a sinner.

2. Understand that as a sinner, you deserve death.

3. Believe Jesus Christ died on the cross to save you from sin and death.

4. Repent by turning from your old life of sin to a new life in Christ.

5. Receive, through faith in Jesus Christ, his free gift of salvation.

MATTHEW 28:16-20

Now the eleven disciples went to Galilee, to the mountain to which Jesus had directed them. And when they saw him they worshiped him, but some doubted. And Jesus came and said to them, "All authority in heaven and on earth has been given to me. Go therefore and make disciples of all nations, baptizing them in the name of the Father and of the Son and of the Holy Spirit, teaching them to observe all that I have commanded you. And behold, I am with you always, to the end of the age."

ROMANS 10:14-15

How then will they call on him in whom they have not believed? And how are they to believe in him of whom they have never heard? And how are they to hear without someone preaching? And how are they to preach unless they are sent? As it is written, "How beautiful are the feet of those who preach the good news!"

ACTS 10

1 PETER 3:15

In your hearts honor Christ the Lord as holy, always being prepared to make a defense to anyone who asks you for a reason for the hope that is in you.

LUKE 9:26-27

For whoever is ashamed of me and of my words, of him will the Son of Man be ashamed when he comes in his glory and the glory of the Father and of the holy angels. But I tell you truly, there are some standing here who will not taste death until they see the kingdom of God."

ROMANS 3:10-12; 23

As the Scriptures say, "No one is righteous—not even one. No one is truly wise; no one is seeking God. All have turned away; all have become useless. No one does good, not a single one." ... For everyone has sinned; we all fall short of God's glorious standard.

ROMANS 6:23

For the wages of sin is death, but the free gift of God is eternal life through Christ Jesus our Lord.

ROMANS 5:8

But God showed his great love for us by sending Christ to die for us while we were still sinners.

ROMANS 10:9-10; 13

If you confess with your mouth that Jesus is Lord and believe in your heart that God raised him from the dead, you will be saved. For it is by believing in your heart that you are made right with God, and it is by confessing with your mouth that you are saved ... For "Everyone who calls on the name of the Lord will be saved."

ROMANS 5:1

Therefore, since we have been made right in God's sight by faith, we have peace with God because of what Jesus Christ our Lord has done for us.

ROMANS 8:1

So now there is no condemnation for those who belong to Christ Jesus.

ROMANS 8:38-39

And I am convinced that nothing can ever separate us from God's love. Neither death nor life, neither angels nor demons, neither our fears for today nor our worries about tomorrow—not even the powers of hell can separate us from God's love. No power in the sky above or in the earth below—indeed, nothing in all creation will ever be able to separate us from the love of God that is revealed in Christ Jesus our Lord.

Who told you about Jesus?

Is there someone you know you need to tell about Jesus? Share this with other people to encourage you and pray for you.

What is your greatest fear in sharing the gospel with others?

ADDITIONAL RESOURCES FOR SESSION 10
AVAILABLE AT DISCIPLESHIPPROGRAM.ORG

Credo House
House
PUBLISHERS

www.credohouse.org

Made in the USA
Lexington, KY
16 September 2013